777

THE BLUE VELVET DRESS SAYS I TOLD YOU SO.

Publisher Contact: hello@bytheseven.com

PRODUCT ID 00073910338203847

http://heidiwong.org/

www.bytheseven.com
published by 777.

If you have any issues with quality, delivery, or
content and would like to report it directly to
the publisher, please visit
www.bytheseven.com/feedback.

Printed in the United States of America for
distribution
worldwide. Contains English & French. Avail-
able through
 retailers worldwide in Hardcover, Paperback,
 and Ebook formats.

graham,   isaiah,   jordi

alana,   ali

annalise

savannah, chris.

CONTENTS

so you want to write like me

get yourself sick
wear your family 's regret like a thousand dollar prom dress
puke your life out onto a black '49 typewriter

there 's never been any
magic
here
only open wounds
with no intention of getting better

i don 't know much about poetry
but i have learned
the true difference
between a poet and a madman

while a madman pays to control her sickness
a poet gets paid
to become her sickness

9

HEIDI WONG

home country

i politely asked my first home not to kill me
so she handed over a roof of iron nails
a bed of needles
threading in and out of my abdomen
years later i am still trying to see how that
too
helped me grow

split my blood
between the seawater of victoria harbor
and the streets of saint petersburg
let beijing separate my bones from muscle
cartilage from tissue
give one eye to pennsylvania
the other to clinton
leave my heart for fifth avenue

10

my second home and i remain on nodding terms
her beauty unquestionable
her smile
unquestionably soulless

if you go back far enough
i am both
the native girl leaving her burning village behind
and the white man she is running from
which is to say
you cannot teach my body to stop fighting for
and against itself

continues

HEIDI WONG

my third home is dirty and promiscuous
strutting down spiral staircases in fake designer shoes
socks mismatched
she's raw rude and unafraid
hair in knots
i want her trash filled neighborhoods
rusty walls like chipped nail polish
the way her silhouette hugs the sweltering sky
but one day i must shed her like milk teeth

every time i make art in the language
that pushes my mother tongue deeper into my skull
every time i sleep soundly in a city
that cannot pronounce my birth name
the earth beats me black and blue
until these bruises
start to paint the flag
of a country that does not yet exist

11

HEIDI WONG

summer eight thousand miles away from you

i think you liked the way i raised hell with each syllable
ruined
reckless splashes of red
on canvas oblivious to color

i think you liked the way
i was the first name
that took your whole body to pronounce
that i reminded you of dizzying
terrifying freedom
a brand new convertible and a tank full of gas
that you could compare me to anything but rosewater

still we dug out each other's rot with teeth
smeared them on white walls
till they resembled childhood

12

i tell you my aunt died drowning in kindness
yet retained a fire beneath her face
i tell you within my scars are the endings to stories
she never finished writing
i tell you that is why
i will never finish writing
you tell me about the boy who can't walk anymore
you tell me how loss paints our skin differently
how there's a craziness behind my skull
you can't seem to reach
i tell you my eyes look nothing
and everything
like all the women before me

continues

HEIDI WONG

THE BLUE VELVET DRESS SAYS I TOLD YOU SO.

knowing you have a tendency
to press your soul to my mouth
just to whisper i don't want you

i raise hell with each syllable
i take whole cities to pronounce
i am terrifying freedom
i am every woman who came before me
spitting art in unison

god bless the months that pulled me away from you
the miles that stood between us like a third body
god bless my mother's attitude festering in my stomach
my grandma's tongue sitting pretty in my throat
swearing in verse at every move you make
god bless my hands
for snapping me back into the world
because of no grandiose betrayal
no public revenge
other than the realization
that generations of women
have burned down the houses they built
for men who never wanted homes
to train themselves in the desperate act
of unloving the unavailable

the only child

my parents will die before me
and i will scatter them into the south china sea
watch their rigidness soften with the waves
because my mother's claustrophobic
and can't sleep in that dark place underground
and my father would want to be with her
i won't move the coffee maker for ten years
won't put away their winter shoes from the doorway
scrub the wine stains off the tablecloth
i will want to kiss their opaque hands
feel my heart expand like a sponge full of blood
lie in the furnace between their lavendered bodies
like i used to when the nightmares were bad
and the cousin who never learned my name
will wait outside
preaching about different gods
western gods and asian gods
the same ones who couldn't
stop her mother's cancer from growing
after a few hours i will crawl out like a newborn baby
go back to the home
that is not a home
talk to my dead brother the way i spoke to god in middle school
to stop the cancer from growing
tell him it's his turn to be the only child
to know how they like their coffee made
their favorite brand of winter shoes
and we will sit in the whole house that is now one room
reminding each other
with the voice i stole from him in 1998
how a child is nothing but an organ
that when carved from the body
can choose
to survive on its own

14

HEIDI WONG

pianos in heaven

when you died i was writing a love poem in america
about how some boy took all i could give
called it too much
heard the chemo stopped working two months later
through an offhand comment in the airport

now i see you in that box
not unlike the crib
my future daughter will sleep in
and accept
i must carry our last name
like the lingering scent of family
haunting an empty home

i wore the dress
i would've kept for my college formal
to your funeral
asked god or whoever
if everything ends
why do i still expect you to show up at my front door

do you remember how i played your favorite clayderman song
on the black piano by the living room
drew with my aunt's lipstick on magazines

now with you
in that box
a body stagnant in sunlight
yet i'm happy for you

continues

16

HEIDI WONG

so i hope there are pianos in heaven
orange ginger tea
and you find her someday
the way you remember each other
stealing candy from vendors
skipping class
holding her unscarred hand down your old neighborhood
like you did in the sixties
looking both ways as you cross the streets

HEIDI WONG

don∙t look
three ghost stories

1. six months after
my friend died two floors above my bedroom
he told me
write the book
go back to california
give her a chance

2. every hospital bed is my uncle∙s
every bowl full of his favorite duck soup
that ten years later
he said tasted no different from the chemo
every vein flattened
every voice a reminder
of his
leaking from the slit of an almost closed door
hospitals are filled with sick people and death
that∙s no place for a kid
take her home
get on the plane
i want her to remember me as i was
not what is left of me

3. i tell the boys in 14a with my mother∙s tongue
the night i
snuck into her room
when the air moved backwards
and the dark scratched at the floorboards

don∙t look don∙t look don∙t look under the bed
don∙t look at the dust shifting through the blinds
don∙t look at the faint fingerprints on the windows

continues

HEIDI WONG

most of me returned to this body
but if you listen hard enough
switch off the lights
you'll hear a shard of my shadow trying to unlearn
how to stop bleeding
into everywhere it once felt safe

19

onion skin

the kitchen smells rancid
as she sits
hands
covered in scars
peeling a rotten onion

pour
salt in my wounds
make them shine like gold
lay your mark on everything

she sits
old scars
kissing new knives
peeling
off the lie

as the illusion falls to the geometric tile floors
like stale onion skin
leaving ink
stuck in her fingernails
your words
shriveling in the summer sun
and the whole room
drenched in a crawling acidity
that used to taste
like honey

milbank 14a is two minutes and a lifetime away

tonight i'm the dust on the windowsill
in a room someone else lives in
a room
a borrowed space
a body housing multiple minds at once and not at once
the moon bleeds light on my limbs and
the new boys don't see the skin i shed between these walls
the fly screen opens if you twist the upper and lower right corners
just you wait
if you turn off the lights and
shut the blinds my initials might still glow on the ceiling
left to dry
from the night
i could do nothing but paint myself into the world
i think my old bones still live there
i think they're growing into the ground
when i come home i'll hear them talk beneath the floorboards

when i come home they'll still be asking where i've gone

21

stars
in memory of isaiah

last night i traced the hallway you lived in
and something in the way it curves
like a broken spine
reminded me of the emergency room in beijing

did you know we could barely see the stars in beijing
so a few weekends
when i was eight or nine
my parents drove two hours from the city
and there
those shining white specks
decorated the sky like
blotches of glowing paint

my favorite thing to do then
was point out my chubby fingers
and draw in the sky
connecting each star with another
binding them into a silver web

my parents saw my thin brows
fiercely concentrated on this
imaginary masterpiece
said that's how they knew
i'd be an artist one day

continues

when i found out what happened to you
i wondered
if i could've made you see
if i just spoke loud enough
wrote
violently enough
could my words bring you to that emergency room
could you lie down with me
in that baby blue bed
could you watch their faces
etch themselves into your mind

because i can still unearth the exact pulling in my gut
the moment i opened my eyes again
saw what i did to my mother

and i want you to feel it
the shattering in her lungs
seeing me
bandaged and stitched like a rag doll
i want you to touch the bags hollowing her eye sockets
see your friends
spilling onto the couch
incapable of anything but
staring at blank walls inching closer
i want you to remember
new york's heart
ripping out of her chest for you

23

continues

HEIDI WONG

when i found out what happened to you
i wondered
if i could 've made you see my hands
pointing up
connecting each
seemingly alone speck of light to the next

we are glowing in our own right
isolated in bodies
in flesh
unable to perfectly describe
how we hurt as who we are

but i 'm not saying we can always find meaning
behind the way we feel
i 'm saying our place in each other 's lives
will always feel meaningful

i traced the hallway you lived in
and something in the way it curves
made me look up to ask the sky
would you have stayed
if you knew
nothing
could ever make the space you used to occupy
seem whole

24

when you meet your daughter

i glued the pair of earrings
i left in your room last september on a
3 0 x4 0 canvas
turned them into art
but what about the rest of it
what about the sheets i threw out because of the blood
what about the blood
what about the months and the months and the months
the moments that
looked pretty on paper
almost empty movie theaters
almost touching hands
opening a bottle of andré in a black velvet dress
what about the person who's still in that room
because every time a man looks me in the eye i am still
in that room
my earrings on the side of your dresser

i knew i was losing myself
when i agreed to let go of the world
and make space for you

it took me nearly a year to realize
you should've never asked me to

once again your scent haunts the barren hallway
we both must take to go home
yet someday
not now
i'll play ghost better

continues

HEIDI WONG

i'll be the ghost dripping through your windows
like moonlight
i'll be the kind of terrifying
short circuiting your memory in a hallucinatory flash
every time you try
to wash yourself clean
i'll be the name
acidic and stinging
lingering in your mouth
as you tell your daughter
to have fun and carry pepper spray in the same breath

someday
not now

i want you to see me in her eyes
when she runs into your arms
earlobe torn
skirt ripped
and know
that once i tried to keep myself safe too
and couldn't

you'll stop calling me crazy the moment you hold her
her cheeks a soft rosy blush
skin milky fresh
pure and untouched

but then again weren't we all

HEIDI WONG

dreamgirl

wu zetian
the empress of china
sits on her throne
holding an empire in her curves
aphrodite walks down the streets of brooklyn in a
skin tight
red latex dress
her thighs sending a quiver through the earth
her heels clicking on the concrete

across the dinner table i hear my dead grandmother say
how little of my brother's face i was able to retain
across the ocean i hear my ancestors whisper to themselves
look at her
the way she moves
our name weighs too heavy on her shoulders

28

when my mother aborted my brother in the 90s
his face was already burnt into my image
an idea
i could never live up to
a ghost
not because he died in our arms
but because we dreamt him into existence

which is to say
almost two decades before i met you
he
taught me
i could never be your dreamgirl

continues

THE BLUE VELVET DRESS SAYS I TOLD YOU SO.

a perfect bite sized beauty
a silhouette robbed of every gorgeous curve and dent
every pound
every inch
cut
into a delicate matchstick
ready to be lit aflame

venus paints herself this time
with her rounded hips and cellulite
twisting into lightning
lacerating the sky

i stand thick framed
built like a masterpiece
positioned
dead center
on a priceless museum wall

look at me
in all this unwelcomed glory

look at me
i am not only
too intimidating
too large for your taste
i am larger than life itself

look at me
why should i want the silhouette of your perfect girl
when i was born with the iconic figure
of a queen

continues

HEIDI WONG

THE BLUE VELVET DRESS SAYS I TOLD YOU SO.

look at me
my power will not be rendered fragile
i was not created easy to swallow

venus
paints herself
this time

turn on the lights
see me the way my god
intended

my hipbones carry the pain of generations
my stretch marks are constellations
connecting thousands of silenced blistering hearts
my belly
a haven
for all the art that's yet to take their first steps

this is for the girls who refuse to be someone else's dream

can't you see
their words disguise the fear
that if they came closer they would disappear inside you
can't you see
they could never contain the world like you do
can't you see
within us
lies the insatiable appetite of every woman
who's been told to stomach their truths

HEIDI WONG

HEIDI WONG

ugly

you tell me i am ugly
that my hands are rotten from the chemicals
my hair plasters over my spine like tree bark
my waist is cinched like a clenched fist
that my eyes carry the remnants of a war zone
my skin is a ruptured dynasty

when i was born my mother named me after the ocean
not for its serenity
but for the dark places no one dares travel to
the creatures mankind has yet to discover
where the pressure bursts your eardrums
pulls the breath from your chest

which man wants to lie
with someone who can choke the truth out like seawater

you say i am too heavy to touch
singed with too much grieving
even by the shoreline you smell smoke
but now it's you i grieve for
this weight fuming within me
cremating to poetry

my mother named me after the ocean
yet i know
i came out of the womb painted
in the colors of a firestorm
for a reason

continues

HEIDI WONG

i am ugly
i am the embodiment of everything you·re afraid of
i am a stunning kind of contradiction
a debilitating honesty
a body
made of shattered organs that still play in perfect tune

so go dream yourself a dollfaced toy
it was my mistake
to ever think your heart was big enough
to hold
both the drowning and the flame

HEIDI WONG

love

if we dissected every closed cut
we carved into each other out of love
reopened
their rosy stomachs to the circulating air
we would find the reason
the heart of a bullet
too
fractures when piercing flesh

HEIDI WONG

THE BLUE VELVET DRESS SAYS I TOLD YOU SO.

in a parallel universe we are more than borrowed time

and now i step back
into the limelight
poetry leaking from the cracks in my armor

i'm losing the memory of how i loved you
i'm losing the memory of how
i would've traded the shine
of every universe
for the quiet world you held within your eyes

HEIDI WONG

i have felt but never been alone

when you cracked open my chest like a glow stick from summer camp
watched my childhood drip down your fingers
i thought of sitting by the dinner table
hands crossed
waiting for the tray of
freshly deboned fish to leave the kitchen

this poem started speaking
in the coffee shop where you scaled me to the bone
made me confess
when i craved for the world to beg at my feet
you reminded me of peace
yet she's a smooth river and you are the ocean
i am a thunderstorm sculpted in stone

the same painting hangs on concrete walls
even the ghosts can't recognize us now

my tongue wants to yell
look at me
on that silver plate
olive oil reflecting off my marble belly
even as a bruised lung i glow
look at me
when you touch her
do my guts smear all over her body

but my empty chest still feels like lightning on its own
my words still have a way
of stripping me to the soul

this poem speaks
in the coffee shop where last october waits in a metal dish
glistening in next summer's sun

continues

HEIDI WONG

and i hear the future
laughing at how i'm letting this haunt me

look around
as long as i have these calloused hands
there is music
art
poetry
there is something i have yet to love
and love in solitude

3939

the blue velvet dress says i told you so

the way i felt with you for a second
robbed my poetry of her voice
but don＇t get it twisted
i＇ll smoke this poem down martin＇s way so you
won＇t have the satisfaction of reading it

nature made it so
love for a man is the release of his burden
love for a woman is to carry their burden
in her chest in her stomach in her slit open smile in her
my heart is flooding
out of my eye sockets but here＇s
your morning coffee exactly how you like it

born to a place where everyone craves
everyone＇s counting
the kind of security your arms give
the way you tell me without telling me without knowing without
meaning to
life itself
is enough
i will never find after these years

so i clung to you like dust
the mauve undertone of an old family photograph you can
no longer recognize the faces of
every time we laid in steel blue sheets
until i＇m forced to be myself again

continues

still i refused your jacket when it was raining
still dreamt
of the piece of me
happy with simply
being
because in reality
your home is a woman and a house and children
the feeling of contentment that to me is a prison
and i was born to swallow the world
until she's forced to believe she's mine

maybe that was your purpose
to tell me without telling me without knowing without
meaning to
just because someone saved you
does not mean you need to love them

41

a tumor on my ribcage
and the fact that we are no longer talking

i tell the doctor just cut it out
make the incision on my left side
three inches below my breast
remove the parts
that don›t breathe in sync with the rest

this is the last poem i›ll write about you
but who am i to control the voice of another living entity
the way it bulges outward
attaches its swollen limbs to mine
makes a home of my blood

what else is to be done
except retreat
into the world i built before you waltzed into it
into old family photographs
steel blue sheets
into the tip of a pen
curved like the blade of a scalpel
and cut you out of my narrative

knowing
this is the first pain
i cannot write my way out of
because it is our story
not the person before me
i cannot let go of

you walk with your head held high
eyes glazed over
holding your body like an apology

i tell the nurses i don›t care about the scar

even in the end we are together
learning
to live with the kind of grief
that hardens flesh to stone

HEIDI WONG

forgetting you

cut my hair because you liked it long
burn my paintings because you wanted them shown
stop the words from flowing

instead i'll
let you read these poems
stay quiet
let the world speak

as far as they know
there's not one photo proving we met so
maybe we didn't
maybe we're fiction
maybe we're a poem not worthy of being written

forgetting you is a part i've played before

at sixteen
waking up next to
lumpy white lines
spilled across my arms
feels exactly
like seeing the empty space where your car used to be parked
when i walked home
alone
moss covering your
sideway skid marks
like skin
growing on top of an uneven scar

45

my friends say he won ʼt talk to me because i ʼm scary

then don ʼt
when did i say i wanted a quiet burial ?

i am not the kind of forest fire that looks pretty on postcards
you think they all watch for nothing ?
i ʼll burn you alive

46

HEIDI WONG

daughter

my mother sent her only child into the world
dripping in blood and grief
covered in the ice of those russian winters
she endured as a girl
smeared in the embers of a battleground
her mother called home

so how dare i allow the memory of a man
rust into my collarbones
gut itself into my pupils
when i am the last of my line
the only heir
to wear my family name like a crown of thorns
biting into my hairline

you call my light too much
yet cannot turn away
don›t you know i was born to blind men like you
who›ve gotten too used to
dousing gasoline on soft petal love
don›t you know disfigured compassion
looks no different from rage

i kiss my solitude on the mouth
i am growing fully
into myself
a serpent swallowing its own tail

my mother let a wildfire crawl out between her legs
dripping in blood and grief
not to please
but to make sure
in this lifetime
the world will witness
the emperor as a woman

48

HEIDI WONG

alternate universe in which i never found poetry

1. my aborted brother turns in my mother's womb again
as i wait with a cup of long jing tea
for him to come home
and reclaim the face stretched over my skull

2. the mid length black dress slips off my shoulders
silence rolls down my spine and
pools on the concrete ground

my uncle and cousin step back into their car
disappear for another decade
and we are no longer standing at the funeral
watching strangers peel clementines
calling her professor

3. the iv bag overflows
blood runs back into pallid flesh
the pills reappear
i start eating healthier
in case my dead aunt needs a bone marrow transplant

4. every story i've lived is a gray sky
lukewarm bath water
a comfortable flame

5. my friend cuts himself down from his dorm room ceiling
straightens his neck and walks into the dining hall
wearing that same button down shirt
we talk about grad school and museums and leaving this town
i never discover the kind of grief that pulses like stanzas

continues

HEIDI WONG

6 . blood runs back into flesh
pills reappear
i pass by my reflection at the airport bathroom
in a country my family does not belong in
and can ›t feel my hollowed chest
missing the cancer that grew in hers

7 . i let pennsylvania watch me grow up
and feel no guilt

8 . when another woman says she carries the weight
of what happens to us all
in different places
from different hands
the thing that happens to every woman
someday
not now
we ›ll play ghost better
someday
not now
he ›ll see us in the shape of his daughter ›s irises
in her laugh lines
in my body i find no place for these words

9 . something in me
that started burning the day i knew of language
still fills the room with smoke
but never speaks to me

recount of last night's dream

and suddenly i'm thirty
living with a partner in the city i love
still dreaming of you as the age we were when they found you
a tall
fragile sparrow
neck cracked purple
wings dangling like electric cords

and suddenly i'm thirty and you are both
the boy in bryant park with ice cream drips on his dinosaur hoodie
and the white haired man in a leather wheelchair

suddenly i'm thirty and it's been september for eleven years
i'm standing outside our home
watching the light in your room flicker on and
off and on and off and on
until it goes out for the rest of its life

even when dreaming i say nothing
even when dreaming i do not save you

so every morning
since the earth did to your bones
what waves do to seashells washed ashore
i've carried my silence like a cross
let it bite down on my shoulders
dig into my spine

because with poetry i can raise you from the dead
but cannot give you back your laugh lines
your grandchildren's voices
cannot make the ground
give you back to us

continues

HEIDI WONG

because all the words i never said
still
cannot amount to the weight
of too late

HEIDI WONG

our summers

i want to show them
how your sun
melted
into pennsylvania's wounds
so they'd understand
why even when the spotlight shines
i will always dream
of the soft orange glow
that quietly led us home

i hold our summers
in the palms of my hands
those glowing little bodies
alive
in bolted
coffins
and whisper
go back to sleep
don't worry about the world

no matter how hard they try
they could never
rebuild
what we had

and neither can we

55

HEIDI WONG

until the fly screen breaks

when i came home
our old front door was covered in a
brand new
silver fly screen
one
barely visible mosquito
caught in its web
fluttering her helpless
broken wings

tried to use my keys
the ones dangling around my neck from when i
lived here
second floor
room with mint green walls
yet the doorknob refused to turn

so i stood with the weight of what's been done to us
unable to understand
still
how two parts
created to complete each other
can become so
incompatible so
quickly

raindrops dripped down my shoulders
slicing open the years like skin
stretched across lavender veins

my legs are weak from the running
and my spine is bent from the pain
but i will flutter my tired wings in circles
move this pen
as long as i can

and repeat i love you in different words
until the fly screen breaks

HEIDI WONG

HEIDI WONG

writing poems about you

when i was walking along
the street i saw
a moth
fly into a
fire and
out and
in and
in again with her
weak little burnt
wings
tirelessly
every time
and felt relieved
that i am not the only one
who chose
to live
like that

she says he'd love her if she were skinny

i stomach the weekend like a bad dream
and i can't tell her
if i puke i might feel like a goddess again
i mean have you seen so much power drip down
rotting nails and
acid coated lips
a voice shaking through her seventh grade english presentation

my dead aunt puts her famous rosemary chicken in the oven
the worms behind her skin eyeing my wounds
she smiles in her brown fur coat like she did in 2008
i remember calling her beautiful on her deathbed
after the chemicals peeled the woman off her bones

i was told that pretty girls should always be soft
small
skinny
compact and complacent in saran wrap
yet all our lives we carry the burden of
too much

as if this new body
scarred and stretched and glorious
still resembles a crime scene

pretty girls should always be soft
right
like the piece of rosemary shoved down my throat
growing into a spine

60

HEIDI WONG

HEIDI WONG

impossible women

and for a second home was a bruised lung
a fractured bone
my mother's tea kettle
my freshman year shower shoes
the acid wash denim jacket from the night market in hong kong
throwing salt in my eyes as a greeting
everything everything everything
reeked of leaving

did you know spiders can regrow their limbs after
they're ripped off their bodies
when my aunt had her double mastectomy
she did not tell her family
did not tell her eight year old niece
only kissed her long brown hair
said
breathe in as much of the world as you can
sometimes we regrow ourselves in different places
from chest
to heart
to head

we impossible women
descendants of uttu
for a second
for a second were convinced
you'd spun us into submission
yet if we asked for truth
could the weight of our story fit between your rotten lips

continues

HEIDI WONG

THE BLUE VELVET DRESS SAYS I TOLD YOU SO.

i was a fire and
i'm still a fire without your tinder
hell cannot catch up to me

you thought your leaving
would take everything
now the devil kneels to my poetry

under our old staircase i hear it echoing
my name kicking in your mouth
like a hundred seething spiders

you thought my love was hard to swallow
try forgetting me

HEIDI WONG

irreplaceable

i remember once
finding cadmium red in my bottom eyelid and
never questioning it
listen
have you tried drinking turpentine because you
wanted to see
what it felt like to be
what you made
listen
i say
for the love of god
leave paint in my
skin my clothes my hair my bones the inner corner
of my bottom eyelids i want
to feel it
build up in my chest like a storm
swarming in my mouth like
tiny mosquitos in the summer
you said
maybe if this
art thing works out i
guess i ll
give it a
try

i remember once
on a sunday
when new york was still warm
you whispering
while twirling a black lighter
between your second and middle finger
how you wanted your art to heal
those around you

continues

THE BLUE VELVET DRESS SAYS I TOLD YOU SO.

i want my art to hurt me back

so i'll let these colors swell
until i can no longer contain them
and you'll drink your morning coffee
oblivious to the fact

we both saw art in each other
but one as irreplaceable
and the other
as just a hobby

HEIDI WONG

dreams

the air feels cold again
like it did when we
walked across the curved crossroad and
left winding footprints
buried in blinding snow

the earth seemed to be peeling off her color then
folding the summer back into her freshman suitcase

now the days we›ve spent
rise within me like a storm
tell me
does she know the way you twitch in your sleep
can she recognize how you walk
from a darkened silhouette moving miles away tell me
who
else
knows the exact way your tone changes
when you believe wholeheartedly
in everything you›re saying
and are still lying

because i›m convinced
with every part of my being
a woman knows when her man cheats

continues

66

she knows it in the space within her chest that splintered
when she feared to be
yet was
proven right
in the pit of her stomach where she might've held your future
in the hollowed arena of her ribcage
that will never stop grieving
in her spine which her mother cradled
shielding her
from what the years could do
in her pulse which her daughters will feel in sync with theirs
in every woman that came before her
trying desperately
to scrape through the dirt
love is here
we say
despite my aunt blaming herself when he
stopping coming to her chemo sessions and
spent a little more time with the girl who had
flowing ebony hair
despite my best friend crumbling in the kitchen
scrolling furiously on a static screen to find what she
must've been missing
we want to believe i
want
to believe
love exists
even when we see only her absence

continues

HEIDI WONG

so i'll let her bruise her knees on your bed frame
the way i did
saturday night
after the rock concert by a band we both listened to in middle school
and i won't
through subtle glances and unpublished thoughts
reach for her hand to say
i know i should hate you but i just
don't

i know he's a dream
only a dream you never want to wake up from

when the blood seeps through your mattress and he
struts around campus like a hunter
adept enough to kill an animal
with one shot to the head you
won't want to wake up when he
makes you question if your voice echoes too loud
emotions appear
too ugly
too disproportionate
too monstrous to fit into a doll sized body you
won't want to wake up when he
shaves off the rebellion in you
mounts a submissive smile in its place you
will not want to wake up

it's always easier to rest in comatose
than to stand and fight alone

continues

68

HEIDI WONG

yet sometimes we fear loneliness so much
we'd put our pain on hold
to hold someone else's world together

did you even notice
when i prepared a meal with my own flesh
so you wouldn't go hungry
just to hear you had already eaten

here
love
you have the spotlight now
and still no one knows your name

i'll wield poetry as a weapon
scar the manhattan skyline
i'll be ugly
disproportionate
monstrous
strong
stunning

once
i was clean and delicate like december snow and this
is what you did to me

october in the rain

placed within the compressing space
between existence and nonexistence
you are the way prozac made me unreal

yet i still ran to you in the rain
hair sticking on my neck like black leeches
the sound of wet muck staining my mother's boots

most of the stars tonight are dead
and i want to hear
from you
what they are shining for

dance around my past like a bonfire
she'll let you leave her for someone less difficult
less alive
while her skin covers
just a bit more of my bones each night

so keep saying i was nothing
yet when he
a part of us both
sent himself back into the earth we held each other
like muscle
tight enough to squeeze out all room for remembering

keep speaking
with a mouth full of bees
knowing
in no way can i say
i did not ask for this

most of the stars tonight are dead
tangled in an endless sheet of opal waves
clean and hurting bodies
grieving for him and you and me and us

your words want to heal my wounds
your actions justify them

HEIDI WONG

this summer

it's time to admit
my heart can no longer fit
in the palms of your hands
and my thoughts have grown too tall
for your sky to keep safe

but if you're still listening

let me be the vines
climbing up your red brick walls
spilling by your sidewalk
so when i
wrap my arms
around the place we called home
it'll still feel like
i'm holding you

72

HEIDI WONG

lafayette

next time i walk down the streets
we used to call home
i 'll make sure
to unzip
my old winter coat
down to the chest

to let
the ghosts
back in

HEIDI WONG

howl

when i was seven
i adopted a dog
who ran away in the middle of the night
to her old home
that did not want her anymore

found her sitting by the stone steps
where a kid from last summer
fell and bled onto the curved sidewalk
saw her fingers laced into the soil
her hair spread across the lawn
loyalty
eating her
from the inside out

some memories are like old dogs
that i cannot put down
and every night before i sleep
i still hear them howl

74

my old clothes

there's a box of my old dresses by the staircase
some spilled on the floor
tiny sleeves and necklines
small enough to be a doll's clothes

from the side window
a light comes on
three figures move in the neighbors' house
a shorter shadow
quivers in the cold as i
feel a lump
in my throat
and a familiar chill
arching my spine into
a submissive angle

so i go back to the typewriter
light a few candles
stare back into
the empty windows

and in its reflection
a porcelain doll
in the size of a girl
turning her pain into something
she can finally hold

HEIDI WONG

unbecoming

the fish
who has lived
her whole life
inside the fishbowl
with 11.5 million
other
fish
became poisoned
with
the monotony
and leaped
landed
on the marble floor
felt the red hot sun burn
her scales down
to the core
as i pack my bags
fold my life into
these boxes i
feel
the circulating air slowly
closing up
my gills
poor fish
suffocating fish
as if
unbecoming a pet
is the same
as becoming
a person

77

HEIDI WONG

masks

there›s something heavy
on my eyelids
something pinning
the sides
of my lips into a
perfectly curved
line

there›s a voice
and two butcher strings tied
behind my head
i›m fine i›m fine i›m fine
convince the kids
it will be alright

the airplane departs
circling the sky
smelling for blood

secure your own mask
first
before helping others with
theirs

78

HEIDI WONG

anxiety

my beautiful stillborn wears
the saccharine aftertaste of prozac like
chanel number five
likes to curl up in my arms
intertwine her violet fingers with mine so tight
sometimes i think they're
a part of my body

she eats my blood so beautifully
i think it might be art
she eats my blood so beautifully
i think she's a parasite
more myself
than i am

she goes off to school
with packed lunches
and those neighbors
see my face in hers
notice
how we have almost
the exact same features

as i dim the lights
go back to bed
curtains
drawn
another minute
taken
watching the world
call me a fool
for thinking i had
any control
over what i have created

HEIDI WONG

how i became an atheist

even my dog
a child who once
worshiped
its owner's presence
knew to stop
shaking
the metal fence
around my front yard
the day it noticed
i
no longer
had anything
left
to feed it

81

HEIDI WONG

creativity

the college newspaper says another artist killed herself
spilled out on her
split double dorm room floors like
sangria from a bad night

all i know is this
the mountains upstate make my lungs feel lighter
their blinding snow scrapes the gold off my skin

all i know is this
i labor in the studio hypnotized by a dream
pressing against my skull
a low buzzing
a hunger for you
and you
and you
to see what i cannot find
in myself

all i know is this
the one you 've grown to love is not me
the one you want to hate is not me
closer
but not me and there 's
no medium
to capture how

the only way to lose the art
is to become the artist

all i know is
some deaths never make it to the papers

HEIDI WONG

THE BLUE VELVET DRESS SAYS I TOLD YOU SO.

burlesque

they like the smell of butchery
the sight of crimson flesh
so you stand
kitchen knife in hand
masterpiece in the other
proclaiming
here is my blood
here is my art

ladies and gentlemen welcome
to the most extravagant
strip tease
down to the bone
down to the soul

here is every one of your regrets
smeared across a white stretch canvas
here is your nostalgia hanging
on an exhibition wall
can you recognize
your heart
in the spotlight
in a stranger's living room
in a magazine
on the big screen

art has never been
the gentle sweep of a brush
songbirds in the spring

art is a hand
that forces humanity
to confront its own shame

art is passion made public
a knife
that keeps its victims smiling

HEIDI WONG

THE BLUE VELVET DRESS SAYS I TOLD YOU SO.

sparrow

how do the sparrows know their way home
how do they know
to return every summer
where they belong
a few days early or late but always
when the sun is pouring crimson

we were the sparrows who waited daily for flight
through storms and floods and the wind
that tore our roofs off
with a flick of the wrist
through winters that sometimes lasted
all year

we were the sparrows
guaranteed the world for our immobility
and continued to fly
because we knew we had our own

there 's a new generation now
and they 'll sleep on our beds
complain about how the floorboards creaks
and not notice our names
engraved into the wallpaper
they 'll sing with the voices
ripped out of our lungs
and learn
to bottle moments in memory

here 's to those young birds
from a sparrow
who has lost her time to fly
here 's to your youth
your loyalty
your fire
for they will bring you to your family
the same way my mind
guides my thoughts back home
as my fingers shape these words
even now

HEIDI WONG

sparrow pt. 2

how do the sparrows know their way home
every summer
where they belong
when the sun is pouring crimson
did i always have something in me
aching to be yours

guaranteed the world for my immobility
i continued to fly
our same route
turning gold to blood to art
as if i couldn't see the windows
the walls the electric
fences
as if with you i'd forgotten
how to be afraid

one last time
to the young birds
from a sparrow
who loved you like a child
unknowing of warmth

sleep on my bed
learn to miss the way those floorboards creak
do not notice my name
engraved into the wallpaper

i hope
to you
they stay glowing golden beams
as they did
when i remained
unknowing of hurt

continues

HEIDI WONG

87

THE BLUE VELVET DRESS SAYS I TOLD YOU SO.

take what they've taught me
here
are the lessons
woven within strings
imprisoned safely in moments
here are the parts of our history
that still look like those photographs

here are my wings
take them home

i've got new ones waiting

HEIDI WONG

resurrection

the winter pennsylvania was torn from my future
i watched the light of childhood
shift
one last time
gasp for air
as if underwater

that winter i swore
the seasons stopped changing

now in this silent hotel room
in the glow of the lampshade
in the shadows overlaying the pillowcase
in the heat of my own breath
i feel
something familiar
beginning to swelter

89

even after they found my friend swinging from his ceiling
i kept looking for him
kept trying to paint the crescendo of his footsteps
the day the cancer lowered my aunt into the soil
bolted her coffin shut with prayers
i traced the silhouette of our city
until the sky was all i knew of her pain

our stories still manage to bleed
out of my fingertips

one last time
speak to me
as if underwater
pour yourself
back into this world

it is always summer
somewhere

HEIDI WONG

deer in the fire

when an animal screams
as she is being roasted above an open fire
we do not call her brave

when the sadness leaves me paralyzed
it is not bravery
but instinct
that carves me out of bed
that pushes me to speak
to walk
to breathe

in the distance a bird flutters her wings
one last time
as her spine meets the cleaver

a deer peers out of a forest lit ablaze
even as her world
turns to ash

will the flames entomb you
or wash you clean
will you blame the fire for its burning
or consume it

when there is nowhere else to run
when your home falls to your feet
the only thing left to do
is endure

HEIDI WONG

collar

out the window
a young girl
kind smile hair down
to her waist
walking
her rottweiler
fur black
as coal she
drags
her
by a leash
imported
from another country

i see her
every day
on empty streets by familiar
buildings
in mirrors
but she
never looks up
changes pace
keeps moving

i see her
every day
the way her smile
bleeds

the dog has a home
there is an address
a street name
a number
engraved on her collar

the girl
nobody knows
for sure

HEIDI WONG

pass on

when you tell me to choose between being myself
and being a good daughter
i'll think of the day i embody
everything i hope to become
so brainwashed with success i forget to come home
the home like a mosaic of shrapnels

and in that moment
i'll realize my future is not my own
but a piece of flesh to pass on
the way mother birds vomit food into their children's mouths
to make sure they eat

i must shove my dream down the throat of my unborn child
pushing hers
to the pit of her stomach
fermenting in its youth
tasting only of guilt

until she gags up the remnants
of everything she hoped to become
steeped
in the scent of too late
for her children to swallow like bedtime stories

identities in this
cyclical game
a mere conglomeration
of who our ancestors failed to be

so when you tell me to choose between being myself
and being a good daughter
i'll think of how
i am not a child of god
because i refuse to swallow his dream

continues

92

i hear the hymn yet can ʼt make a sound
daring to mold my thoughts into existence
instead of turning yours to poetry
daring to bleed
even if i didn ʼt create this body
to bleed from

HEIDI WONG

collision

i want to hold the space
we no longer occupy
as if it could wrap around flesh
and remember sitting on gray stone steps
overlooking the yard
kids playing four square
lights
music
unscarred knuckles

today my universe passed by like a stranger
afraid to make eye contact
and i
laid down the summers
biting into my shoulders

you made me real
once
now put our stories
back to sleep

our mere collision
against
all odds
was a miracle

94

HEIDI WONG

forget the song

when your name fits better
in the mouths of strangers
it sinks

the idea of being an artist
has singlehanded killed off more art
than the lack of inspiration ever will

i know what the fire feels
like
still
on my skin evidence
remains
ash stuck in teenage fingernails
that've refused to grow out
stubborn with their teeth

every morning time sweeps
a fragment of memory off your body
convinces your bones the world is once again
soft
like it was
before what happened to you

it seems
in these inescapable days
it's twice the battle to keep these scars
than to receive them

HEIDI WONG

peaches

she was chosen for all the right reasons
warm golden exterior
blushing red
sweet with a hint of acidity

bring her to your place
peel
off the skin
chew the meat until you reach
her hardened
core

which you cannot
bite through
and you will not
try to

so throw that beating thing
into the basket
next to the empty coffee cups
dirty napkins

and reach for the next one

stockholm syndrome

how curiously protective we are
over our own sadness
how we cradle it like an infant
how we glorify the same souls
who once kept us in chains

beijing
when there are no more scars to reopen
no more hatchets to bury
i wonder if i will miss the way your hands feel
around my neck

i may never find safety under these sinking roofs
but if i am the mosaic
you are the tile cutter

i would not exist
if never broken
by you

97

HEIDI WONG

leaving for new york

the tulip we bought from the market
cries to me
with the kind of hysteria
not unlike the sound of city borders
drowning a fourteen year old

she would have died by her own will too
attached to whatever she finds real
yet she leans
against a polished vase
a barricaded womb
as decoration
for a room that does not need her

i never believed in your gods
only the way
airplane windows swallow conversations
acidity in the air

when the words leave your mouth
they think with a mind of their own
alive in their mutilated bodies
as do children

there 's no blame
in those who want to mold another
in their image

still
i speak to the tulip
fermenting in her juices
cut
with one surgical strike to the stem
wishing she were plastic

HEIDI WONG

from a hotel room in prague

when poetry flows can you hear
art chewing the metal bars
drooling on the floor

sculpting imprisonment
can make it pretty
glowing
marketable
make you
pretty
glowing
marketable
famous
maybe even
happy
it will not make you free

wag your tail in the direction of success
train yourself in their eulogized tricks
could all this gold
make you agreeable

i was never in pain because of the art
art grew in me because of the pain

when you blame this suffocating air
on a city
that never intended to keep you
notice
your thoughts have always been the leash
hungry for a dog

99

HEIDI WONG

after

telling your stories
triggers more pain than healing
more questions than answers

after
tear stained diamond rings

bury the paragraphs
put down the pen
unwind the stubborn words that refuse to speak

there are some scars
only you need to remember

fame

a butterfly leaps
into the sky
dreaming of her cocoon

HEIDI WONG

meeting a reader

i'm walking them
up and down the avenues tonight
their
dark fur reflecting each
blade of moonlight
like a mirror

did i tie the leash too close to their bulging necks
i know what they'll do
when they run out of room to breathe i know
from what they've done
every day
since i opened my front doors
let them in
they were smaller than
tiny paws with
stubby nails
jumping around playfully
like noisy children

a young girl
comes up to me
excited with a smile
that could've ripped her mouth wide open

asks to pet them
holds their crooked claws in her palms
sees only beauty

continues

THE BLUE VELVET DRESS SAYS I TOLD YOU SO.

so i let them do all the talking

if the rest of you
can find beauty in their violence
beauty they shall become

after the girl walks away
says
thank you
i kneel down next to them
to make sure
the leash
is just tight enough

so the poems
can ›t escape
me yet

HEIDI WONG

drown

the second worst part
was selling myself for the numbers
letting them drown the open hearted girl
for a statue
who can sometimes
write like me

the worst part
was that nobody noticed
the difference

simplest advice

as days flash by like
shadows through a train window
it dawns

as flowers open their necks for slaughter
it dawns

as ambulances sing ballads in the streets

it dawns
it dawns

when you have no one
write as if the world will hear you
when you have the world
write as if no one will hear you

.

initials

it's easier
to snap a world
into existence
when you can be a hero
an artist and
a nobody
in the same night

someone
allowed the gods
to keep their anonymity
i just wish they didn't
have to take
mine

10 :54 pm

you remind me of my favorite sweater
from seventh grade
the one i still keep folded
neatly in my closet
even though i know
with perfect clarity
i could never
fit comfortably into it
again

.

the poem is a dog

the poem makes scrambled eggs and
two hot coffees with
no sugar
the poem throws stones
in empty apartment
windows
the poem is allergic to shellfish
the poem smokes her dad's old cigarettes
the poem is a dog
who has chewed through her leash
the poem wakes up for school
the poem sits by the typewriter
the poem picks up the pen
the poem writes
the poem writes
the poem writes herself to life
as i sit here
paralyzed

108

spin

there 's a spider outside
spinning his web
waiting for another feeble fly to aimlessly
wander in
lie down
decide to stay
and as he readies his venom
for her compliant little
veins
i tear off
the last strand of silk
glued to my skin
and remember
the days when i
too
did not seem
to mind

109

HEIDI WONG

shaped like alaska

when you come home
turn on the lights
do not make a sound
ignore the fact that
you do not live here anymore
let your fingers
trace those moments
sunken into the floorboards
try not to wake the family
sleeping in your room
there ʼs a
spot shaped like alaska
on the left side of the drawer
from when you
tipped over your nail polish remover
two years ago
had to move out for a night
cause the smell left teeth marks
on the light gray walls

when you come home
turn on the lights
do not make a sound
ignore the fact that
the scar you left behind
is the only thing
this town has
to remember you by

first time listening to the killers since last april

one of the coldest winter days last year
i was eighteen and blooming through the snow
our first real conversation was about music
and a killers song
that reminded me of what it means to be young
under starry skies that seemed
to never stop glowing

now
i wonder about the next girl
the one who makes up for my loudness
harshness
the one whose hair remains untangled
skin porcelain smooth
the one whose mouth can ʼt raise firestorms
won ʼt spit the kind of truth that cuts deeper than a memory

112

when you smell the night in her perfume
will you mold her silence into acceptance
cause i still feel that night like the air creeping through your old room
a poem i can ʼt peel from my lungs

i grew up listening to the killers
i had that
before you came in my life and
you took it from me

now
it seems like common sense
that there ʼs no love in a smoke filled dorm room
but no one comes into the world knowing that

continues

HEIDI WONG

THE BLUE VELVET DRESS SAYS I TOLD YOU SO.

eighteen
blooming through the snow
i had
her
and you took her from me

the label you so desperately fought to be free of
did not matter
every woman has seen the image of her sisters
stuck like leftovers between a man ,s teeth
i was good for you
and you were hell for me

so tell your female friends i ,m
crazy
overreacting
a little girl with the tendency to blow things out of
proportion

and i ,ll show them
without a word
my hollowed chest

the bullet holes you shot in me make a constellation
yet you stand
loaded gun in hand
crying over the blood stains on your shirt

HEIDI WONG

his old room now has a sun on the wall

i wonder if the girl who lives there now
found my skin from last year dangling in the closet
the only thing left
after the room was scraped clean

maybe i'll see her wearing it down the streets
maybe she'll look a bit like me
placing a tube of pink lipstick on the desk
lying down
drifting in and out of
flashing fluorescent lights

they say
show me where
on the doll
i say in the gap between the bed and the window
where my rose gold hoop earring fell
the drawer where his dark brown scarf used to sit
i say the piece of the wall missing
from the guitar poster he ripped off
folded up neatly and
sent home after graduation
alongside everything else he
folded up neatly and
sent home after graduation
i say the orange blinds that never closed completely
the white dust sprinkled on the curved lamp
i say the place where i feel the image of hands
his and not his
still
solidifying like a tumor

continues

HEIDI WONG

THE BLUE VELVET DRESS SAYS I TOLD YOU SO.

how long did i live on that ceiling for
how long before morning comes
because when the light dims every room looks the same
and i'm
lying down
drifting in and out
counting specks of shadows on uneven concrete
watching the stretch marks on my hips twist to barbed wire
pretending i could ask his mother
if she
too
carried the carcass of a memory in her stomach
so someone else wouldn't have to

THE BLUE VELVET DRESS SAYS I TOLD YOU SO.

when he moves back to manhattan

i will not know why my fingers shake in crowded places
or why if i hadn›t kept the poems
i would remember nothing of being eighteen

i can picture the skid marks from your mother›s car
as you dare to leave
knowing now
and if not now
the day you hold your daughter
how for you forgetting is as easy
as folding that night in your suitcase and
driving

a gaping hole on campus
where all this anger
cannot find someone as deserving to project onto
all this body
strung up and left
dangling from the tree outside our old home

i want my words to force you back into that room
because i am not finished with you yet

when you move back to manhattan
i will search for the hurt
let it devour me
rename the night
as it drips down my spine
as anything but your hands

i will wear poetry as both perfume and armor
notice
that despite how hard you tried
to rid my world of color
the art is still here
and i am still here
to become it

continues

HEIDI WONG

i will walk into a new room
choose a shade of wallpaper reminiscent of
yet entirely different from
the green we used to love

when you leave
i will build a home from the skeleton of the last
and i will no longer think of you

HEIDI WONG

pseudonym

with each stanza
i smile this pseudonym out of my wrists
untangle her
from silk tied tourniquets
and remember

no artist works
to be a master of their craft
only a victim to it

HEIDI WONG

every summer after this

i wrote my first poem
sitting on the curved ledge by your front porch
collecting words from the spine of your sidewalk
finding stanzas in the blood
glowing from your street lights

i called you home when you warmed my fingers in the winter
i called you home when your name seared itself into my neck
when touching you meant leaving a layer of my skin behind

because by your side has always been
my favorite place in america
because your smile is the new year lights
that mark the skyline
all year long
because you gave life to something
within me
that ›s still beating
even when you ›re gone

i ›ve been sitting on your front porch for six years
like this
circling the fragile nape of old ghosts
smelling their lingering perfume
replaying the voices of a group of kids in a borrowed room
singing
off pitch
out of tune
the wrong words
singing until our throats burned and our ears bled

continues

120

THE BLUE VELVET DRESS SAYS I TOLD YOU SO.

you had no flesh around your soul
no bones to keep you standing
no arms to hold me
yet you were the realest love of my life

now
as our story gasps for her last breath
take my hands away from this mutilated machine
and show me
where every summer after this goes
show me how to lay a full stop
on a poem that is
a place that is
a heart

that still
does not seem
dead

HEIDI WONG

dragonfly wings

they cut out her lungs first
then breasts
then blood

so watch this new sun bleed ice
and do not pity me

when i stepped out the gates of my elementary school
and saw the doctors take my aunt apart
like schoolboys plucking out dragonfly wings
she just laid there
bandaged and stapled and glued together
saying jiāo jiāo
i didn·t need those parts
the things we love come back to us
in different forms

but i was there when god remade summer in your image
peeled the silk from your golden street lights
gave them to my blackened youth as medicine

now the same god
will let your red brick walls rot with stories
we are too far away to hear
will leave the windows of my childhood toothless

i was the one who left first
yet for the past three years i only knew sleep
because your heart
still fed light
into the curve of someone else·s irises

continues

HEIDI WONG

THE BLUE VELVET DRESS SAYS I TOLD YOU SO.

watch this new sun bleed ice
and do not pity me
i've kissed the necks of cities that want to hurt me
painted with colors that fill my nails with gunpowder

there are many homes i thought were forever
until i was bombed out of them
until i walked across the pacific
carrying the hollowed space where a piece of my flesh
was removed with surgical precision
and woke to my body
still fighting for its next breath

today
pennsylvania died and took summer with her
and i am left praying
to a sun that burns blue
let the cold
someday feel just as warm

tomorrow
i will wake to my aunt's violet arms
fiercely clutching her concaved chest
saying jiāo jiāo
we don't know what we can live without
until we must

HEIDI WONG

finding a note i wrote to myself in 2015

"the day i know i am not myself anymore
is the day i stop making art about you"

tell me what pennsylvania feels like
how her clothes ripple like river water in june
as she lies
next to that metal can of cranberries
festering in the sunlight

now i still got friends who want my words quiet
say stay focused on the bad
smile so wide for decay
something's
gonna start rotting in those pretty bones of yours

i say let them rot
let them sting like sixteen years of isolation so you
can smell the smoke radiate from the stanzas
do you feel like me yet
you don't recall spending three hours in a teenage bedroom
peeling into yourself but
do you feel it yet

remember what pennsylvania felt like
how her clothes rippled like river water in june
and let them have her
let them lose her

so the loss will also
almost
kill them

this is how i will save your world
not by telling you it gets better
it may never it may never it may never

continues

HEIDI WONG

THE BLUE VELVET DRESS SAYS I TOLD YOU SO.

because when the future spreads herself out like a pulsing bruise
you won›t decide if it gets better
you will decide if you
get better

HEIDI WONG

Heidi Wong is a poet and painter who creates
works that reflect the human experience with an
especially feminist touch. She published her first
work of poetry entitled Sixteen her junior year of
high school, and has been active with
philanthropy since then.

Since posting her work online, she's gained a
worldwide fanbase of over 250,000 followers on
Instagram. This second collection, The Blue
Velvet Dress Says I Told You So, features poetry
and artwork created over the last three years.

Heidi creates and resides between Beijing,
Hong Kong, and New York.

For a special, high-resolution edition of this book
and merchandise, visit www.heidiwong.org

INDEX